God
Trumped
the US and Us with
Hope

God Trumped the US and Us with Hope

BRENDAN KELLY

God Trumped the US and Us with Hope
Copyright © 2019 by Brendan Kelly. All rights reserved.

No part of this publication may be reproduced, stored in a retrieval system or transmitted in any way by any means, electronic, mechanical, photocopy, recording or otherwise without the prior permission of the author except as provided by USA copyright law.

The opinions expressed by the author are not necessarily those of URLink Print and Media.

1603 Capitol Ave., Suite 310 Cheyenne, Wyoming USA 82001
1-888-980-6523 | admin@urlinkpublishing.com

URLink Print and Media is committed to excellence in the publishing industry.

Book design copyright © 2019 by URLink Print and Media. All rights reserved.

Published in the United States of America
ISBN 978-1-64367-986-0 (Paperback)
ISBN 978-1-64367-985-3 (Digital)

07.08.19

Dedication

I want to thank those who have prayed for me to overcome cancer.

A life changing experience that I find an inspiration to write a book.

I want to thank God for guiding me to surpass the challenges in my life.

And to my family for their unending support and love.

Introduction

This book is an update and re-publication of my previous writings. I got moved to write my second book one night as I was about to fall asleep, with a note that this word was my key. I thought I wasn't sure of its meaning but was assured that I knew. I got up and looked for it in my dictionary but it was not there so I Googled it and there it was just as I'd thought. This word became the start of a new book. I'll reveal the word and explain it in the first chapter.

I'm going to introduce myself here. I believe in God, this is all my opinion. I feel that we can't change the past but we are responsible for our future through our actions and inaction's. God provides everything we need. I see myself as being on a tour bus but I'm not driving, just pointing out what seems important.

I live in Seabrook NH where I served two terms as a Selectman 2007-2013, I was also Chairman of the Libertarian Party of NH for two years. I ran for Congress twice without fund raising and only got 17,000 votes. I spent most of my life as an Agnostic but was converted by the life and works of Dietrich Bonhoeffer. Late in 2017 I thought that I had the flu and called my doctor's office, they told me to go to the ER. Within ten minutes they had me on Oxygen and off to the hospital. Two days later I went home with Oxygen installed in my house and notice that I had COPD, Prostrate and bone cancer and a heart valve abnormality. I spent most of 2018 in recovery.

SOB's in Congress

Sorry it's not exactly what you may have thought. Eight years ago, or so, I came to a point in my life where my eyes were opened to Christ and I now pray daily and read my bible. I explained in the introduction how this word came to me as the key to my direction. The word was bloviation and my understanding was that it was about long-winded speech often of a political nature. Bingo! This now made perfect sense to me and I now had the key to explain one of our major problems. We have these seats of bloviation representing us in Congress. What are they doing for us and how do they keep getting away with it?

In the Congress there are two political parties. More important, there are two pools. In one pool are the career bloviates, they are in Washington to enhance their career and go along to get along by continuing to play the game. The game is nothing counts except getting reelected. You do this by making several speeches each year, pandering to the people of your district by claiming you are working hard on the issues that are popular with those voters. Your district thinks you are great, it's the other five hundred who have to go. So, we reelect our representative and he or she gets right back in the pool with all the other bloviates wading around up to their ears in BS and patting each other on the back and reassuring them how great they are. All talk and no action here.

This brings us to the other pool, that's where the action should take place but truthfully there is little positive action taking place here either. There isn't enough happening here to get their toes wet. Representatives and Senators who choose this pool are shunned, ridiculed and ignored. No committee chairmanship for you and little support from your party. We the People, sit at home and wonder why nothing gets done in the Congress. They can't help themselves and they can't change their behavior because they would have to admit that they are and have been one of our major problems. I see a serious problem with both compromise and political correctness. I see compromise as an agreement of each side to overlook the faults of the other to make it appear that they have reached a good agreement. The truth is if both sides are overlooking what's wrong with the agreement, we are better off without it. We don't need anything that can't stand on its own merit.

We have leadership and media that are both comfortable with avoiding any conflict that might bring light to their dark side. The concept of political correctness seems to be that we should never point out anything that may hurt someone else's feelings. I'm sorry but we're not all perfect and we are doing no one a favor by accepting or overlooking their short falls. The proper thing to do is kindly bring their faults to their attention in a loving way and help them overcome their mistakes.

I'm going to use my bible to explain my view on our problem. The basis for my fundamental belief often comes from what I have learned at bible study.

This is my interpretation of a parable in Mathew 18:23-35. This chapter has a heading "Forgiveness" in my bible and it is about that but I'm finding a deeper meaning that Pastor Main pointed out goes along with it. The story goes that there is a lord who wishes to settle his accounts with his slaves. One of his slaves who owes him ten thousand talents is brought before him. The slave has no means to repay his debt, the lord orders him and his family to be sold along with all their possessions in payment of his debt. The slave prostrates himself and begs for patience and he'll repay everything he owes. The lord of the slave felt compassion, released him and forgave his debt. My interpretation is that the lord represents God and the slave represents us, humans. Now this slave went out and found one of his fellow slaves who owed him a hundred denari, he grabs him and began to shake him, saying" Pay me back what you owe." So, his fellow slave pleaded with him to have patience with him and he will repay. The slave was unwilling to wait and had him thrown into prison until his debt is cleared. Seeing what had happened, his fellow slaves were grieved and reported to the lord what had happened. The lord calls his forgiven slave before him and said to him, "You wicked slave! I forgave you all that debt because you pleaded with me. Should you not also have mercy on your fellow slave, in the same way I had mercy on you?" The lord in his anger turns the slave over to be tortured until he can repay his debt. It ends with admonition that we will be judged on how we treat our fellow man as well. Today we have a major problem with unequal treatment by our Justice Department where they are searching to create a crime against President Trump to cover up their failure to bring equal justice against Hillary because they knew they had control over her but not President Trump.

As I mentioned earlier, I believe there is more to this than a lesson on forgiveness. The lesson, clearly, is we need to forgive each other but what I've seen in this also is a need to understand how to use power and act when you are in a position of authority. I see it as telling us there are consequences for misuse of your position of authority I can't remember a time when I wasn't skeptical. I know when and where it started. I was four or five years old and WW11 was on. The navy had a repair shop a half a block from our house in South Boston. The sailors were very friendly to us street urchins. They gave me a doughnut for me and my sister but told me not to eat the hole. I ate around the hole. My mother saw the partly eaten doughnut and explained it was a joke because you can't eat the hole. All I knew was they fooled me and I had to be paying better attention. This led to trouble in my schooling as I questioned everything. The nuns were not thrilled with me, especially in Religion class.

I hope we all have some goals or ambitions to keep us going. Mine is to overcome the guilt that I feel for my generation having allowed the people to be led down the path of democracy. It has always failed because it's against human nature. I believe almost ninety percent of us are followers and should have no influence on the direction we should take for the best interest of all the people. The people who don't understand that there is no free lunch, have accepted the chains that come with it when the government offers such a thing. So, my goal is to have the best and brightest to band together and stand up to the S.O.B.'s and others that don't represent all the people's best interest and see to it that they are replaced with righteous representation. I've been told by all those in power that my dream is impossible and I'll never get half the people to go along with such change. Our country is proof that a small percent of the people banding behind a just cause could defeat the strongest enemy to our quest to govern ourselves.

Our current leadership will go to any length to hide and distort the truth from the people. As I'm writing this, we are having demonstrations about police brutality because of white police officers killing unarmed black men. The media makes a huge issue of a half a dozen of these incidents. Now I'm not saying there should not be an outcry for this injustice. My question is where are the leaders in the media covering the thousands of black children murdered by blacks? While we're on the subject in the worst crime cities in our country, which is the predominant party and what are they doing to address the problem? If they can't scream racism, they offer nothing but stone silence.

The advocates of big government know they need a large population of dependents and they long ago settled on the state school system to provide these dependents. They have no desire to produce the best and brightest. One low level of achievement suits them just fine.

My original intent remains to write about some of our many problems and possible solutions. Up near the top has to be our debt.

There are many cracks starting to appear. Detroit and other cities are in deep trouble. All the tax payers have departed and just the dependents remain. The government- state and federal, can't bail out Detroit because that would be the first domino to fall.

Once Chicago, New York and California have to face reality the upheaval will be underway.

For the few who know me, thanks for your loyalty. I'm not a career writer but more like a career column writer who never had that opportunity. Life for me has always been about trying to make sense of our existence. How and why are we here? Everyone has and walks their own path. I particularly love Bonhoeffer who put me in a corner and changed me from an Agnostic to a Christian through his words and actions. I've been convinced that we have one main purpose. We're here to serve God and each other. This is my opinion of how we should act politically to best serve our ultimate purpose. It's my opinion that we are obliged to love God and care for and love those who may need our help. That requires more actions than words.

It's All About Hope

It's apparent to me that survival today in the past and future depends on hope. I recall that my dear mother when hearing one of us hope for anything always responded with "live in hope, die in despair". Been thinking of that lately and note her pessimistic view.

She was a child of the depression and never forgot the hard times. I have to admit I've not been overly optimistic for the future of our nation up till now. I've been opposed to government control of anything for as long as I can remember.

My question has always been, "What does government do well"? My answer has always been NOTHING. So why should we be in favor of government doing anything? All governments support their own position of power by keeping the people out of the power loop.

I'm hopeful we the people are ascending on a path to true for and by the people control. Career politicians are aghast at the thought they spent their whole lives climbing the ladder of political corruption and now being so close to the top rungs find out we the people may be about to topple the ladder.

This will be my fourth book if I manage to get it published. My first three didn't get much traction. The first because it probably wasn't so great and the second and third for lack of finances to promote them.

My subject this time is hope. I've just become aware of the influence of hope on our life. We are truly nothing without it. Why do anything without hope of success? Hope runs everything that is positive. Despair is in charge of futility.

At this point in my life I'm trying to come to terms with the fact that I wasted so much time in my life on things of little importance. When I was a child I didn't have much if any mentoring. I got by on what I learned day by day from my friends of the street, most were a year or two older than I was. When I was twelve years old, I had the distinction of being the highest educated member of my family. Having reached that point I wasn't really interested in more schooling but continued through High School because my parents thought it was a good idea. The only thing important to me was how much money I had in my pockets but had no clue on how to hang onto it. At that point and until I went into the army, I worked every day to keep those dollars coming in but had never learned how to take care for them. I had everything a young boy could want except direction. Throughout my education years the only things I enjoyed were History and debate.

Hope is being able to hold the media and government accountable to us. So here we are the democrats who before the election were so up in arms that Donald Trump might not accept the results are now seeking any means not to recognize the results and the fact that Trump has won. The democrats lost for a reason, incompetence. They choose Obama in 2008 and 2012 with no experience at running anything and now in 2016 they present Hillary Clinton who is the standard for career politicians in that if her lips are moving, she is lying. The democrats and far out liberals are in shock that the people have figured this out despite the media's all out attempt to never tell the people the truth.

I've been on this path for some time and will now include something I wrote in 2008.

"The stock market expanded again and nobody mentioned to the public that the dollars that supported the increase were down about 40% in a year against the Euro. Aren't Euros just printed up like our money? Just how long will we be able to spend ourselves to prosperity? The latest report states that the average American has $7000 of debt on their credit cards. This is on top of the unfunded future taxes the government is saving up for each and every one of us. At the time of this writing the stock market is shrinking in the face of all the bailouts and the Madoff swindle which is only allowed to the federal reserve. Is there any way we can reign in this runaway train before we go over the cliff?

What we need most is a BS free country. The first thing that comes to mind is the elimination of prohibition. In the 1920's we thought it would work on alcohol but it didn't. Now they are telling us it will work on drugs, it hasn't. We've had thousands of deaths and millions in prison because we have a government that thinks its part of their destiny to moralize for the citizenry. Let's give freedom a try as in if you are not doing anything to harm me, I should leave you alone. Has there ever been anything that was prohibited that didn't flourish?

While we are engaged in the elimination of Bull Shit in our country, perhaps we should consider individual safety and just how this issue is handled. Now the present-day thinking would say more police and more gun control. Maybe we should look for a state with little crime now and see what we can learn. Ah, Vermont with the least stringent gun laws has little crime, now that is backwards from what the government says should happen. The reason for this is of course a matter of respect. When everyone is armed you don't have anyone treated without respect. You don't have thugs breaking into houses where the residents are very likely to be armed. Our problem is that our government wants to be able to sneak into your home and keep an eye on what you are doing. Never forget the first move of fascist regimes is the outlawing of private fire arms. A well-armed citizenry is difficult to enslave. If we desire peaceful co-existence each household should have at least one weapon for self-defense.

The founders of our country thought this issue was so important that they made it the second amendment to our constitution right behind freedom of speech. Since then we've had thousands of laws passed that are in direct conflict with the constitution. Now the government interpretation of the second amendment is that only a militia which they claim to be the National Guard has the right to bear arms. At the time of the writing of the constitution the militia was the armed heads of each family and they were armed to defend themselves from unwanted government, the same problem exists today. We have a government that seems to think they are above the constitution and have the right to ignore the rights of the citizens to maintain their death grip on the public trough.

So here we have ample evidence that we have been betrayed by our government and the media they are in bed with. The question is what if anything we are going to do about it? I've been voting for libertarian candidates for over twenty years and became active in the party. The truth is as certain as I am that we libertarians are able to see the truth in our present system, our general public can't. Total liberty appears beyond the comprehension of those who are scared to death of the concept of standing on their own two feet and taking care of themselves. If we can agree that we have to stop this runaway train that will be a start. Without an agreement to stop this pending disaster, reversing it is out of the question.

Personally, I feel paying 45% of your income for government is excessive and I'm confident that each of us has some figure that would be an awakening for them.

REAL WORLD 101

ANTI FREEDOM GOALS

RICH / HOPE TO BE RICH? NEAR POOR / POOR

| 2% | 58% | 20% | 20% |

Obama's plan tax the 2% rich out of existence to help the poor and near poor. Results, there are no rich and everyone is poor except the social leaders who are still near poor. (Welcome to soviet eastern Europe)

FREEDOM GOALS

RICH / HOPE TO BE RICH / NEAR POOR / POOR

| 2% | 58% | 20% | 20% |

Freedom tax plan, eliminate all income taxes and the government programs they fund. Results, the rich are expanded to 20% and are on average seeking to hire five people each so we have.

RICH / SEEKING TO BE RICH / NEAR POOR / POOR

20%   60%   10%   10%

There are one and a half jobs for each person in the field of workers seeking to be rich, with no taxes the charitable organizations are well endowed by the natural generosity of free Americans, leaving the 20% of the population who don't join in the prosperity due to laziness or disability. The lazy are free to join in and take one of the many jobs available at any time they choose and the 10% who truly are unable to join in are easily taken care of by voluntary social programs funded by the generosity that has always been demonstrated by the hard working citizens in our country and the liberal leaning who have always been generous with Other People's Money will have the same choices as the rest of us.

LOGIC

I've had problems my whole life because of logic. I've always had a hard time believing things that were illogical to me. As a child I was sent to Catholic schools where religious training was part of the study. I had difficulty with matters of faith when I was asked to believe in miracles which supposedly happened 2000 years ago. This brings us to modern day religion. We have many different religions today and I feel confident that they all believe that they are the one true faith and would love to convert all others. If by chance one of these is correct, then all the others are not. I am not anti-religious. I feel it is a great tool to raise a moral society which is preferable. However, we must condemn crusades and religious wars of all kinds. We have a government which keeps expounding positions which have no basis in logic. They saw what happened with the prohibition of alcohol. Prohibition started a major crime wave, failed miserably and had to be repealed. With all that history in front of them they still started the "War on Drugs". So far, they have started a major crime wave and failed miserably, all they need to do is end it. We must admit our mistake. We can pardon anyone convicted of a nonviolent drug related crime and send those in prison home.

Another big problem on the horizon is the fact that to many people work for the government. The government just doesn't create any wealth, they only confiscate it from the people who don't work for the government. The tax burden on working citizens is getting out of hand and there appears to be no will on the part of the people to scream in protest. We expect great services from the government and ignore the fact that the government has to rob someone to pay for them. I'm calling on you to look around and take responsibility to get involved with the recovery of individual liberty. Now the government is not going to accept this movement. In N.H. The movement has started with the Free State Project and their Porcupine Party. Once they actually become viable the government will be looking for a reason to crush them as they did with the Branch Dividians in Waco. The government has no intention of abolishing slavery of the citizens. Understand if we re-attain freedom all government employees who don't work in the limited necessary functions of government would have to get a job and support themselves like all the other citizens.

We the citizens of this once great nation have to stop enslaving each other for our little slice of the pie. Everyone wants to cut government waste unless it involves the elimination of some service, we hold dear to our heart. We have to understand that all services are more efficient and cheaper in the hands of private citizens.

I'm not the only one who has been working long enough to see what has happened to the average family over the last fifty years. My family moved to a middle-class neighborhood in 1950, it was our first home. My parents paid about $11,000 for the house. Their mortgage with principle, interest and taxes was $97.00 per month. At that time $100.00 per week was about what each family in the area had to live on. None of our mothers worked outside the home. Nobody in the area paid income taxes because most of the families had two or more children. The exemption for each member of the family was $600.00. With most families having a $2,400.00 or $3,000.00 exemption they would be tax exempt. Now we have to keep in mind a new automobile at that time was about $1,100.00. If the government had continued to keep the middle-class tax exempt the personal exemption would be in the 12 to 15 thousand dollars range today. This is the reason the middle class is under siege in our country today. We have to face the fact that over the last fifty years Democrats and Republicans alike have taken turns in control of the government but the continuous attack on the middle class escalated regardless of the leading party. So, if the tax burden went from 3%

to 40% in the last fifty years in which I have worked, what will the future hold? When the high school grads of today have slaved away for fifty years will the rate be 80%? It will if we don't do something about the way government works today. This pattern has been obvious to me for many years and the traitors we send to Washington to represent us have conspired to take care of themselves and bury the middle class. Anybody who votes for these corrupt career politicians is uninformed or a co-conspirator.

How did we ever get stuck with a government system that provides better services and benefits to the people who live off the tax payers than are available to those who are paying the bills? Why do the senators and representatives have better benefits than the tax payers? These are career thieves, if they weren't, they would have changed this on their own. If Social Security is such a great program why aren't they enrolled? They have been stealing from the public so long they think it's legal.

President Bush landed on Social Security reform as his project to leave a legacy for his administration. He had this idea that private accounts will eventually be a good thing for Social Security, I agree with him. Any money left in control of the individual is an improvement over government IOU's".

OK that's enough of my old thoughts.

Now comes a massive disruption, the people have chosen a new leader with a new direction. A change from we can't do anything to the positive message that we can do anything we wish to do if we work together. Trump talked to real people about real issues that affect their pocket books and he won. There will be a lot of foot dragging in hope that he fails. This leads me to his most important issue which he has not really elaborated upon. This would be "Draining the Swamp". I take this to mean ending the corruption that runs everything in D.C. It's always about the money and what's in it for me.

President Trump has been on the paying end of this throughout his life and knows all about it. He canceled the new Air Force Ones the reason being that all government projects are outlandishly expensive for a starting point.

If there is one thing President Trump is good at, it is drawing attention. In my opinion he needs a private sit down with the leaders of both parties in Congress to explain that there is a new boss in town and he is going to lead in a new anticorruption direction. The new deal is you are with the best interest of the country and the people or you are not and it all starts today. He should inform them he has zero interest in laying blame for past corruption, just the elimination of it going forward. Have those in office accept the new direction of representing the people or resign.

I think about our future based on Faith Hope and Charity. Faith in God and our country to do what is right and just for all. Hope we will all come together to support equality and justice for all. Charity by our new government to be charitable and forgiving of those who betrayed us by their former selfish behavior.

I'm still waiting for the "Truth to Set us Free" from my first book. I have my own concept of truth. We're living now in the 21st century and I hope we believe in justice and equality for all. We have among us some who wish to remain in the 13th century. They have every right to do that but not to try to impose it on others. There are countries that wish to maintain a system where woman are second class citizens, that's fine for them but not in my country. President Obama said we are not a Christian nation and that may be so but we are a predominantly of Judeo-Christian beliefs. Anyone looking to set up a substandard of Sharia law is in my eyes a case of treason and should be grounds for such a charge.

We have had to try to survive eight years of the rudder less ship administration of Obama and it's a breath of fresh air that President Trump will be our new rudder and provide the leadership we need.

Those in government and the media who have joined in deceiving us for decades are naturally in distress over the thought of the country being led by someone who isn't owned and controlled as they have been.

They will eventually get over it if we make it known that we will not be vindictive as they have been toward, we conservative small government people. We should forget the past but crack down mightily on the present and future corruption and selfish leadership. We must call for the dawn of a new era in our U.S.A.

Yes, President Obama we are exceptional and proud of it. You spent many years listening to the trash talk of Jeremiah Wright and just don't understand what it means to be an American. We naturally lead the way to show the light of freedom and justice to the world. They can follow or not but we will lead.

Michelle Obama had the gall to appear with Oprah and pronounce that we have now lost hope. They are perfect examples of well-educated liberals who only talk to and listen to their own kind and so will always remain clueless with regard to real life experience and what it takes to address problems caused by their opinions.

They won't see that the economy has already taken off in anticipation of the new leadership of hope.

My hope is that this is the end of the damnable Democratic party and we just all become Americans. The Democrats have always been the party of division and in opposition of freedom and equality for all. We have them down and must hold them accountable for their actions of the past and not allow them to continue lying to and deceiving the people.

I'm in favor of their current plan of resistance to anything Trump as they won't be causing any further damage to our well-being.

There will be great angst in the heavy blue states. Just imagine the thought that the new president has a phone and a pen and he actually uses the phone to explain what he is doing and his pen comes with an eraser and white out to correct the mistakes of the past.

I'm truly excited over the thought of real budgets where you can only spend what you take in. We've seen what happened to Detroit's population and now there are signs that Chicago, New York and California are facing mass flight of the producers of wealth and leaving just those who are dependent on government handouts behind. These are the places where truth has been ignored and will be experiencing quite a shock to their having to face reality. On the bright side I predict that a decade from now we will have a sea of purple states all with the same unity and direction of what is best for all and the end of political correctness and corruption.

I've been against the Fed and the IRS; my main objection is that they are not American but foreign corporations that control our currency. Thus far they admit that we are twenty trillion in debt and hundreds of trillions in future liabilities that they seldom mention. With new leadership at the Treasury and a ban on future printing money for bail outs of any kind, perhaps there could be some stability. My complaint is that we have no method for encouraging people to save. When banks make loans, half of their profit should go to their depositors as in 3% interest on savings and 6% interest on loans. That could be sustainable for centuries in our country.

As mentioned in my last book we would have great savings with the elimination of the IRS and institution of the "Fair Tax". Everyone pays the same sales tax percent and gets the same tax return from the Treasury. All federal assistance programs other than Soc. Sec. And Medicare would be eliminated. Disability claims should be handled locally. This would require more work for the local treasurer and town clerks because tax refunds would only go to those who are registered residents of their town and deposited in their local bank on a regular basis such as quarterly. Everyone pays in by the same federal sales tax and everyone gets the same tax return. If for example the tax return was $400. per person quarterly that would be $6400. annually for a family of four plus whatever they had earned. I think that's a big deal to those living on minimum Soc. Sec. And the working or not working poor. No more food stamps fraud. No more tax returns being sent to houses outside the country with dozens of families claiming to live there. Let sanity rule. I found it quite interesting that food stamp participation decreased by 1.1 million in Trumps first six months, another clear sign we are headed in the right direction.

My hope is for the remote possibility that they will really address our fiscal mess. I believe this has been caused by over taxation by the government at all levels to provide for the useless bureaucracy that studies everything and resolves nothing. I would suggest that President Trump should look at a list of all the government employees in D.C. And lay off 10% in each department or agency then wait three months to access the results. After the waiting period he would have a report on the effect of the downsizing and strongly consider total removal of any department or agency that was not missed or had their duties taken over by another sector and that could be inside or outside of government.

My favorite would be the elimination of the IRS with the "Fair Tax" making it unnecessary. Along that line with the way things would change, we need a way to collect sales tax at the point the item or service is delivered unless it's delivered outside the country in which case an excise tax should be collected. I'm referring here to the Amazon type internet sales should be required to forward the sales tax to the town treasury where the item was delivered.

We are facing a very tough next two years. President Trump is proposing a thorough house cleaning with his drain the swamp concept. Some will think it's too much and many will think it's not enough. What it must be is a start. Doing nothing is not an option.

If you are about to undertake a total renovation of your home while you're living in it, that thought could be quite daunting and you could resist starting the project. If your house is in really bad shape like our fiscal situation you just have to dig in and get going. The goal has to be the management of moving our government toward equality for all. All subsidies and exemptions must go as in ALL. If you can't offer a plan equally to all the people then it must be eliminated. The concept must be to get rid of all the corrupt extortion policies of our career political class and replace it with equality for everyone. Now that's draining the swamp.

When President Trump gets his way there will be swift change. He seems to be a man with a 20-hour work day and this is why he has always got things done. He will out work most former presidents and especially his predecessor, Obama in my opinion was a complete failure for one simple reason. He is not and has never been an American. The reason Trump won is he talked to the American people who the liberal elites totally underestimated. We the American people will be happy to roll up our sleeves and work even harder for a leader who believes in us. This ends stagnation, onward and upward bound in 2017.

HOPELESSNESS

This is the main problem in our country that has to be addressed. I believe the main cause of the problem is the failure to properly educate our children over the last sixty years. Most who actually graduate from high school are still not prepared to do anything. Keep in mind that 300 years ago there were 13-year-old children who were captains of ships because they could navigate. The goal should be that we ask each child in the second grade what they would like to do when they grow up and start helping them to be prepared to attain their dream. The dream could change and their study course adjusted as needed but raising children with a one size fits all education is a disaster.

Two major problems that I believe are the results of hopelessness are the violence in Chicago and elsewhere. No education and no work lead to crime as the only means of survival. The second problem which has hit home even here in NH is the problem of addiction and drug overdosing. I think trying to escape the reality of their hopeless situation must be a major cause of this problem. So here I sit pen in hand at the beginning of the Trump administration. I'm encouraged watching career politicians trying to vet his cabinet choices who are obviously much smarter than they are. This is my idea of high comedy. I love knowing that these are not the best and brightest we have to offer and enjoy being able to just sit here and watch them prove it. These are the people who passed Obama care without reading or understanding what it would do. Hopefully the replacement will be much better, it could hardly be worse.

ON TO REDEMPTION

We need a new approach and business-like style to the operation of our government. It must have truth as its foundation. We have massive waste due to corruption of our elected officials and some of our government agents. We don't need a witch hunt that is looking to lay blame, just take action to change things moving forward. It seems simple enough. If it's broken fix it. One fix at a time until we wipe out all the corrupt practices. There is something rotten in America and it's one of our lead problems. We are over run with drugs, that's legal and illegal. I'm sick of these TV commercials urging people to ask their doctor to prescribe some new drug to them despite the long list of possible bad side effects. My point is that there is something wrong about ads urging people to ask their doctor to prescribe all these new drugs over any possible holistic cure that may help their ailments. It's always new expensive drugs as the only hope despite their acknowledged drastic bad side effects. We the people must scream for relief from our current pay for play system and a replacement with a system that is all about what is best for all the people.

We are all awaiting the replacement of Obama care. One change that must be looked at is the fact that Medicare doesn't pay for holistic care. I believe the FDA and Big Pharma are in bed together to keep our people addicted to their expensive drugs. It's always about the bottom line and not what's best for the patient.

How about a 100 million dollar fine to any drug company that willfully suppresses a non-drug cure for anything with half the fine going to the person or company that proves it? I'm in favor of a regulation on prescription drugs that limits advertising on them to only those who are authorized to write them. This will fit right in with cutting the cost of health care. Hopefully we can wean our nation off our predisposition for seeking a drug for every ailment.

My simple solution to our fiscal woes is for the new president to be the defunder in chief. Any program that is failing to produce, just cut out the funding. Most government is failing to produce anything positive so we should start every year with a zero budget and fund only what is absolutely required. Mainly the courts the military, the State Dept., Intelligence agencies and send everything else to the states. Have you heard the term non-essential workers? That is the description of 90% of government employees. Do you think there could be substantial savings in their elimination? So, we have a starting point to cure our ills.

I took some time for reading before the Inauguration and picked up "Treason" Newt Gingrich's latest novel. A great read, I couldn't put it down. When I returned it to my library I took out "Crisis of Character" by Gary J. Byrne. Now that is an eye opener. Our country dodged a bullet when Queen Hillary the Horrible failed. I knew that Bill Clinton was an embarrassment as president but she would have been worse. I'm quite happy to be one of her deplorables.

Our media which I feel is generally either clueless or corrupt gave bad reviews to President Trump's Inauguration speech. I thought it was him telling the world that there is a new boss in town and God knows we need one. They talk of his first hundred days. He is looking at the task of undoing the damage that has been done to our country over the past hundred years. No one should expect him to repair that in four years. Just be grateful we have someone who is willing to start draining the swamp.

After reading "Crisis of Character" I'm a bit upset that he spoke so nice to the Clintons but I'm thinking that could have been out of respect for the office which they never had.

President Trump's toughest task will be breaking the century of corruption imposed by our elected officials who have only cared for themselves. Here in NH we have a new governor who is a republican after a string of democratic governors. The previous Governor Hassan is now a member of our all liberal female congressional delegation. The democrats didn't bother to follow the requirement to report monthly on our state budget and it comes out now that our Medicaid funding has a sixty-six-million-dollar deficit. It's kind of mirrors the mess in DC that the President must resolve. Governor Sununu starts right off with a mess to clean up. His predecessors and the democrats in our legislature have no regard for budgets and how they waste the people's money.

One of the largest wastes of tax payer dollars is the government education programs. These were originally designed to provide little learning ability and they have continued their program. Here in Seabrook NH the last time I checked we were spending $13,000 per student per year. We don't have a high school. Private school tuition for middle schools is $3,500 for a better education but just call the school boards out on that and then you just don't care about the children. I just think we could spend that money on something productive like real education where children learn to think not just follow directions.

I thought it was a sad sight to see millions of mindless dupes parading around with their crude vulgar signs and unable to answer questions as to why they were there. That's what you end up with when you take God and education away from our children and their parents. Blind leading the blind.

Our primary goal has to be getting government out of our lives. We should start with the easiest, getting it out of education. It's not the government's responsibility to educate you. That's your parents' job. If you are not educated it's because your parents failed.

The big problem ahead will be when one of the states collapses in default. The cities and states can't print their way out of their over promised positions. We've all sat home in comfort and felt very bad about the sight of destruction left behind by a tornado. The next week it's forgotten by us but not by those who lost everything. We won't easily get over the fiscal mess we face when the next big bankruptcy happens. I don't know where it will happen first. Could be Chicago, LA, Dallas or any other large city but it will cause a domino effect that won't be quickly repaired.

This all stems from lack of equality. We have to understand the concept that you can't get or ask for any benefit that isn't open to everyone. Why should police, fire fighters and teachers be able to draw a pension and retire at 50 when everyone else is looking at 67? There are jobs that many just can't perform at 55 years old and you may have to find work with lower physical requirements. We need to grow up and face reality.

We're all liberals when we are children and living on an allowance from our parents. Most outgrow that when they have to pay their own way. Our problem is that our elected officials are still on an allowance from the government instead of representing we the people. All the inequality and debt problems make up the big blivet which has yet to hit the fan. Thank God we no longer have a career politician in the driver's seat.

Now a week into the Trump administration and he is keeping his promises to the American people. The left is in distress and holding many demonstrations on their wish to resist change and the elimination of corruption. Notably a freeze on hiring has been imposed indicating there will be a reduction of workers in the government through attrition. Many resignations at the State Dept. that covered up for Hillary is a welcome sight.

I don't understand why these blue cities are up in arms about the Trump immigration policies. Even with his wall, he is just upholding existing law. Even building the wall isn't new, just the actual funding of it. The President has a whirl wind schedule with two or three new announcements every day. He will overwhelm the Congress and their snail pace that is used to doing nothing much except to raise more money for themselves and their party. President Trump will be holding their feet to the fire. It's good to see that the campaign wasn't just words and he meant what he said. If the Congress gives up spending 75% of their time on fund raising and spends it reading the bills regarding the changes that the President is seeking, they may actually get something done for a change.

I saw on Boston TV that there was a rally in protest of the new immigration policies. I didn't see any outrage that the legislators voted themselves substantial pay raises. They are resisting any changes and supporting the usual corruption.

I'm reminded from my reading of the word in 2 Timothy 2, this being the second letter of my favorite Paul's to Timothy. He writes in part. 3 "Realize this, that in the last days difficult times will come. 2 For men will be lovers of self, lovers of money, boastful, arrogant, revilers, disobedient to parents, ungrateful, unholy, unloving, irreconcilable, malicious gossips, without self- control, brutal, haters of good, treacherous, reckless, conceited, lovers of pleasure rather than lovers of God".

I feel he was describing our times almost two thousand years ago.

I believe we should give our new leader a chance to turn this nation in a new direction that is more in tune with the rule of God and not the rule of man. I understand the reluctance of the left as I was in their shoes eight years ago. I'm going to take advantage of the fact that after President Obama we're still America despite his best efforts to derail us. This is just my opinion but I've always believed that he is not an American. My suspicion comes from the hiding of all his school records. I know for a fact that he never attended Columbia. Why hide his high school records? I believe he may have come here as a foreign exchange student which would prove he is not now and has never become a citizen. One more thing I question when and where did he register for the draft? OK now I feel better, I got that off my chest so I can breathe easier but I don't know why my doubts haven't been answered long ago. I believe there should be an Obama presidential library and it should be an outhouse by the steps of city hall in Chicago, a special gift to those who wished him upon us.

The governments penchant for throwing money at our problems instead of actually addressing them is the problem. Our schools and health care are prime examples. This change in tactics is a shock to those who are responsible for our current situation but thought they would never be held accountable. The liberals are doing everything they can think of to slow down the changes President Trump is trying to make. Just the thought that they should show up and do their job is a jolt to them. Everything I write is my opinion or position. I'm thrilled to be watching the demise of the democratic party. They haven't learned anything from their defeat this election and will lose all power in 2018. They will be left with a handful of states on the coast and the rest of the country in republican hands. I believe this will happen because President Trump is demonstrating that he keeps his word. When he keeps his word to the black communities to bring education and jobs that the democrats never followed through with, the democrats will be gone forever. Have you ever noticed that the democrats have only one strategy? They throw mud at their opponents and accuse them of all the things they have done. They cannot look back on their accomplishments and take credit because there are none. Obama care and the mess in our inner cities belong to them.

Sanctuary Cities

We have this issue of Sanctuary Cities and now California wants to be a Sanctuary State. I guess I'm not too bright because I just don't understand how criminals of any kind deserve protection from prosecution. Just the why someone who doesn't have the right to be here should be protected from punishment for their criminal behavior is beyond my understanding. Fortunately, there is a solution. When an illegal commits a crime for a second time that does serious harm to a citizen of our country and has received sanctuary city protection in the past then the Mayor of the city which provided such sanctuary at the time of the previous offense should be charged as a co-conspirator in the new crime. Thus, ends Sanctuary Cities, counties and states. I'm entitled to my opinions and reserve the right to change my mind when presented with proof that my opinion is wrong. I'm still waiting.

AWE

I'm truly awe struck with what is happening in our country. I pray often for enlightenment on what I could do to be helpful to my fellow man. I'm rewarded with some idea of explaining how I see things from a religious and historical perspective. With regard to our new President, I was sure early on that he would win. I live here in NH surrounded by liberals. I started looking seriously at Trump when my guy Dr. Carson dropped out and supported Trump. My wife and I got on board. I knew Trump would win because of my wife's friends. There is a group of a dozen lily white mostly widows from 65 to 80 years old. I asked my wife who they were voting for and was told that one was for Clinton and one was undecided but the rest were voting for Trump. At the time we were being told that Trump had a problem with woman but if this group here was supporting him, he would have no problem in the heartland. When I told my friends that Trump would win easily, they doubted it would be easily.

I was awed by the large crowds he drew. I knew who he was but had never seen his TV shows and only saw his speeches on Fox News. The other thing was that this was going to be the year of the outsider. Early in the republican primaries the four outsiders Trump, Carson, Fiorina and Cruz always combined for the majority of the support.

I love American History right from our beginning where the founders believed in divine intervention. There was the first great divide of those who opposed the king and those who were loyal to him or feared him. Washington believed and succeeded as our first and greatest President. In my mind he cannot be surpassed because he is the one who refused to be king. Years later in the 1860's we had our second great divide where the Confederate states wanted to leave the Union over slavery and other issues. The Lord provided us with Lincoln who died for his belief that we had to remain united. I believe that our third great divide is upon us. After a century of the rule of man seeking to eliminate the rule of God we are faced with a great split and the Lord has provided a new leader. Trump has mentioned God more in his first two weeks than Obama did in eight years.

The cause of our current divide is the need to drain the swamp and all that entails. President Trump as soon as he got his hand off his bible spoke to the nation and reiterated his campaign promises and the fact that he intended to keep them. This right in front of the members of Congress who showed up. He doesn't have an easy task. The three branches of our government that are supposed to provide a balance have been in disarray for far too long. It's all become so political and President Trump has been charged with bringing it all back into alignment. The elimination of the corruption that has over taken our government is a daunting task but at least this President is aware of the problem and is not beholden to the elites who control our corrupt career politicians and the main stream media that takes their news from them.

The reason this is such a great task is the great divide in support for the President. We have the ultra-liberal 25% who will oppose anything proposed by the President. Then we have about the same amount of die-hard Trump supporters. The real problem lies in the remainder. Most of the republican establishment are in this group and it remains to be seen if they will in fact give up their former corrupt ways and follow the lead of the new boss in town.

The democrats are doing everything they can to slow Trump down by not getting his cabinet confirmed and this thus slowing the changes he will make. Career politicians are really into slow and the new president is all about charge ahead. President Trump will leave them breathless. I have similar sleep requirements to the new president and I'm really enjoying this.

Do you believe in miracles?

Belief is a great thing and faith can pull you through your troubles. Keep the faith, work hard to get along with each other and look out for each other and our nation will prevail.

We need to convince our elected officials that it's not about them but rather what is best for all the people they represent and our need to be able to trust their leadership.

I believe the president feels he is on a mission to save our country from the corruption of the past century.

One of my blessings as mentioned earlier is that I don't require much sleep especially if I have something on my mind. This has me awake in the early morning hours when C Span shows the congressional hearings of the previous day. I was happy to see a discussion by the leaders in our government agencies and their problem with holding government workers accountable. It was mentioned that there is a problem with the system in that the only way to reward good performance is to promote to a management position. If an IT guy or gal is the best, we have at what they do it doesn't mean they would be equally good at managing others. In fact, they may have no ability outside their sphere of expertise. It was good to see the subject at least being discussed. Why take someone who is happy with what they are doing and change them into something they are likely to be unhappy with? The problem with the government lagging so far behind in the IT field is they are not paying the going rates for IT skills and expertise. I believe we have to many government employees who should have been replaced with a computer years ago. A massive streamlining is in order. This goes for the pentagon as well. More people in uniform and far less in suits. More updated equipment to replace all that is obsolete.

The New World Order

For decades now we the people have been left on the side lines while the UN has taken our generous support but mostly supported ideas foreign to our line of thinking. I don't know what lies ahead but it appears we are approaching a sudden change of direction. We have a new leader who is unlikely to be happy throwing money at anything that doesn't produce positive results. We the people have a serious flaw that must be addressed. To many of us are unwilling or unable to differentiate between rights and wants. The rights we must demand are to life, liberty and the pursuit of happiness. If some of us wish to add wants to this list of rights you must realize you are asking the government to steal from someone to provide for your wish list. This makes you a thief and in support of a government that steals from others on your behalf. This is our main split between the rule of God and the rule of man.

I need to address the great wall on our southern border. Our neighbor to the south Mexico is a sovereign nation. You and I can't just walk in there and say it's OK I'm here because they will rightfully lock us up and deport us. We also need to be a sovereign nation. We have spent trillions of dollars in support of other nations. Why not invest in making Mexico the best it can be? Mexico has a serious crime and corruption problem that partly relates to our drug problem. If we could clean up that mess, Mexico could be the number one vacation destination for many Americans. With a sound Mexican economy many of our illegal immigrants would likely self deport. We are a nation of immigrants and we should continue with that. I don't really know what our policy is with regard to quotas on immigration but feel Canada and Mexico should get preference because of their proximity and the fact that they are not a terror threat to us.

With regard to our undocumented aliens. As we start to round up the criminal elements who are here, we will cause a new problem. It was news to me that there are 950,000 already on the list of deportees. We must examine the choices available to them. They can sit and wait in hope we don't catch up with them or they can self deport and return to where they came from. I believe there will be an enormous number who will continue to travel north and flood Canada with this infection.

These illegals are a big drain on our economy. They will quickly overwhelm the Canadian economy. We need to realize welfare isn't cheap no matter where it's provided and most of these people are not buying health care and are in fact putting hospitals out of business.

For far too long we have had the career politicians and media that has been looking out for their own self-interest and failing to trouble the people with the information that could lead the people to understand that there are consequences for avoiding the truth.

As I've mentioned before my life has changed and I'm on this tour bus as a guide pointing out the sights and events that I notice along the way. We the people have elected a new non corrupt career political person. He said he plans to drain the swamp. For the past century the leadership of our country has been on a bus where they and the media just point out to the public what works for them. We need a change. Now when I speak of media, I'm not referring to those who work in the field of media but rather to those who own it.

I had lunch the other day with our youngest daughter, she is all caught up on God but not politics. She asked me "What's this Trump and Russia thing about"? I explained in my opinion it's a smoke screen like all news provided by the government and media. They want you looking at what they say and ignoring what they do, look over there, not behind you where we've been and still are picking your pockets.

I want to get into what I've seen and learned in my life time and the past century. The great theft starts with the establishment of the Federal Reserve. The big money lenders who controlled Europe needed to get established here so they bought off some of our Congressmen and corporate leaders to represent their interests. They sold the idea to the Congress, selling our freedom to control of foreign bankers. The IRS is their collection agency. They have no authority at all over ninety percent of the people in America. Let's look at who they do have a connection with. They would be people who are in positions of service to the US government, such as Congressman and Federal Judges who are required to pay income tax.

In 2007 I became aware that I'm not a taxpayer. This due to the definition of a taxpayer in the IRS code. In addition to this a broad Federal Income tax is against our constitution because Federal taxes must be apportioned so that everyone pays the same. When the government wants to raise money through taxation it should asses each state according to its population. That's how we did it before the corruption set in.

IRC Sec. 3401
    (a) Wages
        For purposes of this chapter, the term "wages" means all remuneration for services performed by an employee for his employer.
    (c) Employee
        For purposes of this chapter, the term "employee" includes an officer, employee or elected official of the United States, a State, or any political subdivision thereof, or the District of Columbia, or any agency or instrumentality of any one or more of the foregoing.

When reading legal documents, read carefully and assume nothing. Anything not stated is intentionally omitted. If they meant all employees, they would have said so but they can't.

In a 1941 report titled" Collection of the Individual Normal Income Tax".

"For 1936 taxable income tax returns filed represented only 3.9% of the population."

"The largest portion of consumers income in the United States is not subject to income taxation. Likewise, only a small proportion of the population of the United States is covered by the income tax."

So how did they get the rest of us involved? There was the matter of WW11 and how to pay for it. They appealed to the people through the Victory Tax Act. The people were asked to voluntarily pay an income tax for the years 1943 and 1944. This act automatically expired at the end of 1944. This unconstitutional Act was not challenged by the general public who thought it the patriotic thing to do and the corrupt IRS is still collecting.

I know this and now you do. Our elected officials know it or should and their failure to act is reason for their dismissal, hold them accountable.

On to the most expensive issue of the day, health care and what has the government done for us? When I was a child in the mid 1950's the people who had health, insurance got it as a perk from their employer or if you were self-employed you joined an HMO. My parents had six children, I'm the oldest. My father was a fisherman who worked on commission, if he caught fish he got paid if not he didn't. We had no health insurance. In 1955 our youngest sister was born with CP. Both of her ankles were turned out so she wouldn't be able to walk. A couple of years later the Boston Children's Hospital operated on her taking bone from her calf's and putting it in her ankles. She wore braces for several years for walking support. This cost my father $10,000 which is almost what he paid for our house in 1950. I'm quite sure that would cost a million today.

Our problems with expensive health care in my opinion started in the 1960's when the AMA and FDA started regulating and restricting the number of doctors and drugs, thus creating monopolies that supported them and ripped the rest of us off. In 1960 health care cost $27.2 billion or 5% of GDP, in 2015 health care cost $3.2 trillion or 17.8% of GDP. None of this giant increase in cost is about better health care it's all about more government control and less personal freedom.

Here we are and the question is what can we or should we do? Twenty or thirty years ago the popular question was "What would Jesus Do"? The question was seldom answered but meant to have you think about how you are doing things. I have an answer, Jesus would do what his Father (God) wanted him to do. His and our Father wants us to love him and each other. Moses taught us how we should act and Jesus showed us but we still choose man's way over God's way. What could possibly go wrong?

With all the blessings God has bestowed on our nation do we really wish to keep trying God's patience? We have now been Trumped and I think it's about time we start paying attention to what is best for everyone and not just ourselves.

As part of our division I'd like to address those on the left and Bernie supporters in particular. Bernie Sanders has always been a rabble rouser. Among his many mistaken beliefs is his opinion that we can reach Utopia by over taxing the rich. Flash, the rich didn't get that way by being dumb. They are humans and when attacked will try to defend themselves, in this case by moving and taking their money with them. Bernie's idea has never and will never work. Thirty or forty years ago Venezuela was one of the most prosperous countries in South America. Today after many years of Communist socialist rule it is a total disaster. If Bernie got his way, we would end up following the same path to the same results.

REALITY

Have you noticed the long back up lines of people trying to get out of our country? How about all of our citizens who are flying to other countries for better healthcare? This is fake news. On healthcare we are being informed that 20 odd million will lose healthcare under the ACA replacement. They are reluctant to report the fact that 28 million will lose their coverage if it's allowed to collapse. Many of these are now being forced to fund coverage that is wildly expensive and unnecessary in their opinion. Healthcare in our country has become an anchor on the economy. It's not about providing good healthcare but rather more government control of each of our lives. On the issue of coverage on your parents plan until age 26. Adult hood should start at voting age. At that time your parents are no longer responsible for you're on your own. Time for you and our country to grow up. Now if you are a parent who feels that you have failed in the preparation of your children for entrance into adulthood, feel free to help them in any way you choose. We just don't need any government requirements on the issue. We all owe gratitude to our parents for our life and it's beginning years. We have an obligation to return the favor at some time in the future when they may need some help. To me that is God's way and the American way and we don't need any government to remind us of our duty.

    I have to admit that I'm somewhat surprised at the trouble the left the media and some of the establishment politicians are having adjusting to the new leader. I guess they really did believe they could fool us forever. What I've for a long time believed is that we the people know when we are being lied to. President Trump has taken a different path to deliver his message and by passing the main stream media which he doesn't trust. So, we've had six months or so of all Russian collusion stories and nothing reported on the administration's accomplishments. One very important issue is our military and their support of the President. He has kept his promise to fix the VA and to support increased spending on our military. We now have a President that has the military's back and they have his. All his opposition are dragging their feet in hope of slowing him down but he is still charging ahead and urging them to get a move on. I hope the Republicans notice how well they have done in the replacement elections and come to an awakening that they should get fully behind our new leader. This is a stretch wish on my part as it would require many to leave their current path and start walking his.

The first economic domino may have appeared. The Governor of Illinois has vetoed the budget that doesn't address the fiscal woes that the state faces. The legislators are faced with over riding the veto and continuation of kicking the can down the road or making very unpopular cuts to entitlements. They will struggle to borrow their way out given the states credit rating. That didn't deter the legislators from quickly over riding the veto and raising taxes. How do they expect an over 30% increase in income tax on the people and the corporations that employ them to repair the 147-billion-dollar shortfall in their unfunded liabilities? I suspect Chicago will soon be our Caracas and then maybe it will draw the proper attention that we should be paying to the situation.

Here we are six months into the Trump administration with only one news worthy event according to our media, that being the Russians interference with our elections. When the Russians looked at the candidates in our Presidential election who would they have preferred to win? It could only be Bernie the admitted socialist. Our media has beaten this issue to death rather than report on the things that have been accomplished thus far. There was little coverage of the visit to the Middle East where the President called upon our Muslim allies to do more to halt terrorism abroad. I've seen little on the positive economic data that has already occurred. Nothing about the many onerous regulations that have been repealed and Obama Executive orders being overturned.

What we do hear reported and glorified is every violent protest that the left has concocted and these are blamed on the Republicans and Conservatives.

The Congress not surprisingly is bogged down with the healthcare reform effort, this is a perfect example of how difficult the swamp draining will be. Most of our elected officials hold public opinion far above principles and vote accordingly. On what is a sad note to me Congressman Jason Chaffetz R-UT has resigned in disgust. It appears he thought the new leadership at the Dept of Justice would have helped his House Oversight and Government Reform Committee but it didn't and he being of undeniably good character just had to walk away. We'll miss his leadership in the effort to drain the swamp. Thankfully he has appeared on Fox News and is in position to keep the public informed on our corruption issues.

Here we are six months into the people's revolution and what have we learned? The first thing we know is the establishment wants no part of it. The media spent the whole time seeking Russian collusion on the Trumps and no time on Clinton Russia Uranium swindle.

The Dimms (thanks Lou Dobbs) are just sitting on their hands hoping to have the Obama care disaster taken off of their necks and placed on the republican's plate. On that issue the republicans who voted to repeal the ACA all the time when they knew Obama would veto it are now MIA with the president sitting their pen in hand.

None of this is a surprise, it's all about the continuation of the current system of corruption that candidate Trump pledged to end. We the people elected a President who was not a corrupt career politician because we saw the need for change. Those who are ingrained in the corruption will resist change to their end. Democrats and Republicans alike don't charge each other with corruption because they are all guilty and have a long on-going system of turning a blind eye toward bribery and corrupt contributions.

I for one never thought this would be easy but it just has to happen.

We are seeking to change human behavior. The Lord made us all different with our own appearance and abilities. There are those among us who are all about themselves and they gravitate toward positions of power to enhance their own status not ours. We are on a mission of weeding those traits from those we choose to represent us. We gave notice when we elected President Trump. We must now require allegiance to we the people and the new direction from those who would represent our interests. This has to be the main issue in the 2018 elections. I've noticed that there are PAC's with that goal in mind.

As for today, little has changed. We've seen that the FBI is politically corrupt. There was a change at the head of the Justice Dept. but no apparent change in their actions or inactions of our system of justice.

On the bright side there are reports that it will take eleven years at the current rate of progress for the president to get all his appointees through the Senate. Great news for downsizing.

We've had a recent run of new all-time highs in the stock markets. This in part due to belief that we will be having tax reform. If we can actually slow down the theft of government the economy will start to grow and the people will take notice.

The divide we face is becoming more obvious. It starts with the rule of God. We are willing to follow the commandments or we're not. Our current leadership is clearly all about loving themselves with little interest in the well-being of all the people. They are comfortable with a system that fails to inform and educate the people who need it most. Leadership isn't easy or for the faint of heart. If you choose to lead you must be mindful that there will always be some that can't be pleased because they expect you to always agree with their position no matter how one way or absurd it may be.

The President has been involved with our foreign diplomacy in that he actually visits and talks with the other heads of state. Don't want to read too much into this but the fact that we are all talking is a good sign. It appears that our past omission of leadership was a problem that has now been solved.

War is a terrible thing but ISIS had to go and it seems that President Trump has been living up to his promise to eradicate this cancer on humanity.

The deep state media only seems able to report on tweets that are meant to by pass them. Nothing that shines positive light on the President's actions gets any attention at all. There have been constant calls from all sides for him to stop with the tweeting. I ask why should he when they seem to bother his enemies so much?

This to me is the real start to a new world order where the U.S.A. Once again leads. My hope is that we find a way to lead in peace and by example, based on the old style of carry a big stick and have no need to actually use it. My main fear is that we get forced into making an example of someone and that opens up the possibility of a real war. There have always been leaders with little regard to the harm they cause in their pursuit of more power. Just look at the mess in Venezuela where the leadership is all about themselves with no regard for the truth on the damage they have caused to that once prosperous nation. We can't allow anything like that to get started here.

I know that I'm not pointing out anything new. We the people have been put between the rock and hard place for decades. I'm just looking to call out those who have put us there for their own benefit. I just thought about a time in my Libertarian activist days when I had the opportunity to address our local Rotary Club breakfast meeting. It was posted on You Tube as "This is NFG". At the time I wasn't looking at the government as corrupt but simply inept.

We really must start to hold everyone accountable for everything they do and don't do if they are in a position of responsibility for representing our overall best interest.

One of our most important divides is that between our President who is seeking to drain the swamp and those in our Congress who make up a large section of the swamp. He has to deal with many of his own party who are out of step with the direction he wishes to lead us and the Democrats who are taking no steps at all.

At some point the Trump Russian Collusion non sense should come to an end. The AG Jeff Sessions is in a tough spot. He has done a good job on the security and immigration issues but has failed to ignore the long-time corruption of not holding elected officials accountable for their misdeeds with regard to their contributions and bribes that have been accepted and used for personal gain. With Sessions choice to recuse himself in hope of transparency it put the investigation in the hands of the liberal Obama left overs. They appointed the Special Council that Comey wanted and picked a longtime friend of his. No apparent corruption continuation there right!! Just another example that the corruption in our politics is so ingrained that those in DC can't recognize it when they see it.

For six months now all we've heard about is Russian influence on the election and nothing about the Hundred and Forty Million Dollars that a Russian Company donated to the Clinton Foundation after Hillary approved giving them access to over 20% of our Uranium. They spend endless time and energy chasing shadows and no time on actual provable corruption. There in a nutshell is the swamp that needs draining. We the people must band together and insist on the change that would provide us with righteous representation. Those who don't represent our overall best interest must go and be replaced with better non corrupt representation as soon as possible.

We must prepare for the 2018 elections and back candidates who are committed to support the President in his effort to end the corruption in the swamp. With any gains in 2018 we will be set for a Presidential election in 2020 where candidates will either be with the President or not. It's time to cut to the chase. We have a blessing in President Trump and we have to provide him with full support. He is aware of our one main problem that is out of control government. Government is always a somewhat necessary evil but never a solver of problems. We see the horror of out of control government in Venezuela and North Korea but fail to notice that our own is only slightly better. These leaches of career government service don't care about ordinary people, they are all about their own self-interest and not rocking the boat of status quo.

President Trump is the key to open the flood of truth to flush out the swamp of corruption that has been festering for a century in our nation's capital. He will need some help from we the people. We must provide new blood in the form of term limits by not voting for any incumbents. I don't care how highly you hold your Senator or Representative. They all must go because none of them are looking out for anybody but themselves. If perhaps one comes along who is clearly tipping tables over and calling out our massive corruption problems an exception could be in order but there is no one like that there now.

This is our opportunity to do away with the Congress that has repeatedly let us down. The situation that we must address is our current leaders who don't see the lack of equality in our country because they are relying on it as their source of power. We have a country that is all divided up into little special interest groups that think their special treatment is right and just, because it works for them as it works for the Congress. Our new goal must be total equality. There can be no exceptions.

You are not exceptional because you are white, black, brown, red or yellow, male or female, gay or straight, athletic or not and mainly intelligent or not. We all deserve equal rights and protection but never preference. Naturally we are not all the same. Some have more abilities and with that comes more responsibilities. God expects Us to care for the poor and disabled not the government. It's our responsibility to reject all exemptions and subsidies which are the life lines of corrupt government. We must get rid of the Congmess and replace it with a Congress that is totally made up of volunteers who meet twice a year for two weeks and insures that we have a government that provides a strong defense and equal justice to all. Then we will be able to hold our heads high among all nations.

Our country was blessed from the start. We had founders who believed in freedom. They were not perfect and didn't get everything right. They were God fearing and believed in divine providence. Today we have a President who is not perfect but seems to be counting on God's help in performance of his duties. A century of corruption is more than enough. Keep the President and our country in your prayers.

We have been at this attempt of self-rule for 250 years or so and the same problem persists. Can we actually get by without a King or strong Federal government? We no longer have a King but a corrupt Federal government system to deal with. The founders knew of the problems we would face and tried to institute a government that was restrained by a constitution that restricted its power. We are still fighting that battle because those in power seldom are willing to give it up as 1st President Washington did. Fifty years after his presidency he was revered as a saint because even then they knew that walking away from complete control was highly unusual human behavior.

I'm a political and history junkie who is confident in my perceptions of what we are and where we should be heading. At this point I'd like to include excerpts of the opinions of our 1st and greatest President's words from his Farewell Address August 14, 1796.

Profoundly penetrated with this idea, I shall carry it with me to my grave, as a strong incitement to unceasing vows that heaven may continue to you the choicest tokens of its beneficence; that your union and brotherly affection may be perpetual; that the free Constitution, which is the work of your hands, may be sacredly maintained; that its administration in every department may be stamped with wisdom and virtue; that, in fine, the happiness of the people of these States, under the auspices of liberty, may be made complete by so careful a preservation and so prudent a use of this blessing as will acquire to them the glory of recommending it to the applause, the affection, and adoption of every nation which is yet a stranger to it.....

The unity of government which constitutes you one people is also now dear to you. It is justly so, for it is a main pillar in the edifice of your real independence, the support of your tranquility at home, your peace abroad; of your safety; of your prosperity; of that very liberty which you so highly prize. But as it is easy to foresee that, from different causes and from different quarters, much pain will be taken, many artifices employed to weaken in your minds the conviction of this truth; as this is the point in your political fortress against which the batteries of internal and external enemies will be most constantly and actively(though often covertly and insidiously) directed, it is of infinite moment that you should properly estimate the immense value of your national union to your collective and individual happiness; that you should cherish a cordial, habitual, and immovable attachment to it; accustoming yourselves to think and speak of it as of the palladium of your political safety and prosperity; watching for its preservation with jealous anxiety; discountenancing whatever may suggest even a suspicion that it can in any event be abandoned; and indignantly frowning upon the first dawning of any attempt to alienate any portion of our country from the rest, or to enfeeble the sacred ties which now link together the various parts.

For this you have every inducement of sympathy and interest. Citizens, by birth or choice, of a common country has a right to concentrate your affections. The name of American, which belongs to you in your national capacity, must always exalt the just pride of patriotism more than any appellation derived from local discrimination's. With slight shades of difference, you have the same religion, manners, habits, and political principles. You have in a common cause fought and triumphed together; the independence and liberty you possess are the work of joint counsels, and joint efforts of common dangers, sufferings, and successes...

One of the expedients of party to acquire influence within particular districts is to misrepresent the opinions and aims of other districts. You cannot shield yourselves too much against the jealousies and heart burnings which spring from these misrepresentations; they tend to render alien to each other those who ought to be bound together by fraternal affection....

To the efficacy and permanency of your union, a government for the whole is indispensable.... The basis of our political systems is the right of the people to make and to alter their constitutions of government. But the Constitution which at any time exists, till changed by an explicit and authentic act of the whole people, is sacredly obligatory upon all. The very idea of the power and the right of the people to establish government presupposes the duty of every individual to obey the established government.

All obstructions to the execution of the law, all combinations and associations, under whatever plausible character, with the real design to direct, control, counteract, or awe the regular deliberation and action of the constituted authorities, are destructive of this fundamental principle, and of fatal tendency. They serve to organize faction, to give it an artificial and extraordinary force; to put, in place of the delegated will of the nation the will of a party, often a small but artful and enterprising minority of the community; and, according to the alternate triumphs of different parties, to make the public administration the mirror of the ill-concerted and incongruous projects of faction, rather than the organ of consistent and wholesome plans digested by common counsels and modified by mutual interests.

However, combinations or associations of the above description may now and then answer popular ends, they are likely, in the course of time and things, to become potent engines, by which cunning, ambitious, and unprincipled men will be enabled to subvert the power of the people and to usurp for themselves the reins of government, destroying afterwards the very engines which have lifted them to unjust dominion....

Let me now take a more comprehensive view, and warn you in the most solemn manner against the baneful effects of the spirit of party generally.

This spirit, unfortunately, is inseparable from our nature, having its root in the strongest passions of the human mind. It exists under different shapes in all governments, more or less stifled, controlled, or repressed; but, in those of the popular form, it is its greatest rankness, and is truly their worst enemy.

The alternate domination of one faction over another, sharpened by the spirit of revenge, natural to party dissension, which in different ages and countries has perpetrated the most horrid enormities, is itself a frightful despotism. But this leads at length to a more formal and permanent despotism. The disorders and miseries which result gradually incline the minds of men to seek security and repose in the absolute power of an individual; and sooner or later the chief of some prevailing faction, more able or more fortunate than his competitors, turns this disposition to the purpose of his own elevation, on the ruins of public liberty.

Without looking forward to an extremity of this kind (which nevertheless ought not to be entirely out of sight), the common and continual mischiefs of the spirit of party are sufficient to make it the interest and duty of a wise people to discourage and restrain it.

It serves always to distract the public councils and enfeeble the public administration. It agitates the community with ill-founded jealousies and false alarms, kindles the animosity of one part against another, foments occasionally riot and insurrection. It opens doors to foreign influence and corruption, which finds a facilitated access to the government itself through the channels of party passions. Thus, the policy and the will of one country are subjected to the policy and will of another.

It is important, likewise, that the habits of thinking in a free country should inspire caution in those entrusted with its administration, to confine themselves with their respective constitutional spheres, avoiding in the exercise of the powers of one department to encroach upon another. The spirit of encroachment tends to consolidate the powers of all the departments in one, and thus to create, whatever the form of government, a real despotism. A just estimate of that love of power, and proneness to abuse it, which predominates in the human heart, is sufficient to satisfy us of the truth of this position....

In offering to you, my countrymen, these counsels of an old and affectionate friend, I dare not hope they will make the strong and lasting impression I could wish; that they will control the usual current of the passions, or prevent our nation from running the course which has hitherto marked the destiny of nations. But, if I may flatter myself that they may be productive of some partial benefit, some occasional good; that they may now and then recur to moderate the fury of party spirit, to warn against the mischiefs of foreign intrigue, to guard against the impostures of pretended patriotism; this hope will be a full recompense for the solitude for your welfare, by which they have been dictated....

Relying on its kindness in this as in other things, and actuated by that fervent love toward it, which is so natural to a man who views in it the native soil of himself and his progenitors for generations, I anticipate with pleasing expectation that retreat in which I promise myself to realize, without alloy, the sweet enjoyment of partaking, in the midst of my fellow-citizens, the benign influence of good laws under a free government, the ever-favorite object of my heart, and the happy reward, as I trust, of our mutual cares, labors, and dangers.

Note: Here we have our 1st President forewarning us of the corruptible nature of political party. We obviously didn't heed his words and for that reason we have this Congress that we need to address We have made some inroads in that fewer of our people now identify as Democrat or Republican and choose to call themselves Independent. That's not good enough. We must educate the people to stand up for themselves and their liberty by identifying themselves proudly as American. The goal must be equality for all and the elimination of career politicians and the corruption they represent. This is our swamp. They are not going to just walk away, We the people must drive them out of our lives so that we can live in liberty and freedom. It's all about insistence on a government that represents all of our citizens with total equality.

At this point I think it is fitting to insert an excerpt from our new Presidents Inaugural Address January 20, 2017

Today's ceremony, however, has very special meaning. Because today we are not merely transferring power from one administration to another or from one party to another, but we are transferring power from Washington, DC, and giving it back to you, the American people.

For too long, a small group in our nation's capital has reaped the rewards of government while the people have borne the cost. Washington flourished—but the people did not share in its wealth.

Politicians prospered, but the jobs left, and the factories closed. The establishment protected itself, but not the citizens of our country.

Their victories; their triumphs have not been your triumphs; and while they celebrated in our nation's capital, there was little to celebrate for struggling families all across our land.

That all changes—starting right here, and right now, because this moment is your moment; it belongs to you. It belongs to everyone gathered here today and everyone watching all across America.

This is your day. This is your celebration.

And this the United States of America, is your country.

What truly matters is not which party controls our government, but whether our government is controlled by the people. January 20, 2017, will be remembered as the day the people became the rulers of this nation again.

The forgotten men and woman of our country will be forgotten no longer. Everyone is listening to you now.

You came by the tens of millions to become part of a historic movement the likes of which the world has never seen before. At the center of this movement is a crucial conviction: that a nation exists to serve its citizens.

Americans want great schools for their children, safe neighborhoods for their families, and good jobs for themselves.

These are the just and reasonable demands of a righteous public. But for too many of our citizens, a different reality exists; mothers and children trapped in poverty in our inner cities; rusted-out factories scattered like tombstones across the landscape of our nation; an education system, flush with cash, but which leaves our young and beautiful students deprived of knowledge; and the crime and gangs and drugs that have stolen too many lives and robbed our country of so much unrealized potential.

This American carnage stops right here and stops right now. We are one nation, and their pain is our pain. Their dreams are our dreams; and their success will be our success. We share one heart, one home, and one glorious destiny.

The oath of office I take is an oath of allegiance to all Americans.

For many decades, we've enriched foreign industry at the expense of American industry; Subsidized the armies of other countries while allowing for the sad depletion of our military; We've defended other nations' borders while refusing to defend our own; And spent trillions of dollars overseas while America's infrastructure has fallen into disrepair and decay......

But that is the past. And now we are looking only to the future. We assembled here today are issuing a new decree to be heard in every foreign capital, and in every hall of power. From this day forward, a new vision will govern our land. From this moment on, it's going to be America first....

I will fight for you with every breath in my body; and I will never, ever let you down...

We do not seek to impose our way of life on anyone, but rather to let it shine as an example for everyone to follow.

Note: I'm going to make an assumption that President Trump is familiar with Washington's Farewell Address.

Clearly one of our most pressing problems is the existing overload of liberals entrenched in our government who don't realize that they and their disregard for our Constitution is a serious matter.

This traces back to Eric Holder and his too big to fail position with the banks and their not being brought to justice. Rest assured if a bank or corporation is important but convicted of fraud or some other malfeasance there will be a rush to replace them.

There have been reports that over 90% of the government employees at the State and Justice Departments who made political donations made them to Clinton and the democrats. We the people need a change. How could anyone see this and not consider it a conflict of interest? When employed by our government you must represent the best interest of all the people not yourself. We the people need legislation that makes such behavior grounds for immediate dismissal. Another group that has to go are those who refused to turn over Clinton emails to the Congress and others under FOIA. They took a position that the public was not interested as their wall of defense. Knock it down and find a judge who will charge them with contempt of Congress and jail or fine them and certainly fire them as needed until we resolve this corruption.

Well it's a new day and I've had a change of heart. I started with the belief that we could get through this Congress if we were to forgive and forget. That was not a realistic position. I've noticed the great effort being put forth to change our history. Let's look at that. 250 years ago, slavery was universal, we didn't start it we ended it. We had a Civil War and survived it. Thank God. The changes have come slowly but we can still get there.

Here is the hand we have to play. This is not a subtle change it's a revolution and each and every one of us must choose a side. No one gets to vote present. We all must decide if we want to continue the current corruption or drain the swamp.

I thought last night how lucky it is for me as a political junkie to live here in NH, I guess it's the same in Iowa where Presidential campaigns are never ending and anyone interested can get to meet most of the candidates up close and personal. This allows for first impressions which can be quite telling. I've never met President Trump; his crowds were too large for me. Never met Hillary Clinton, all her appearances are pay for view.

Those I met in a positive light include Mike Huckabee who I got to sit with at a picnic table alone for about twenty minutes. There was a rally at a park I think in Stratham NH where the vast majority attending was for Ron Paul whom I'd already met many times. When I recognized Gov. Huckabee alone, I joined him and found him to be open, down to earth and friendly. I don't think he has changed and he is bright enough to support the President.

Another who made a lasting good impression was Herman Cain who I came across in front of our state capital. Also, very open and friendly and obviously very smart. Not a surprise that he backs the President and the changes he seeks.

While on this subject I have a collection, I'll refer to as Pompous Pukes. The absolute founder and leader in my life time was the late not so great Robert Byrd who another member of the club Hillary Clinton admired so much. The current leader of the clan is Bernie Sanders who is already running his 2020 campaign. He saw what happened to the Soviet Union and what is now happening in Venezuela and he's still trying to sell his Utopian nonsense to the American people. Don't get anywhere near Bernie it might be contagious.

As stated earlier I've changed my mind on forgiveness for the major players in our current corruption. The American people have to see the Clintons and their closest allies carted away in orange coveralls. There has to be an example that their behavior is not pardonable. The leaders of the FBI and Justice who covered for them should be charged as well.

OK, I feel much better now. When my Red Sox finally won the pennant, my son gave me a tee shirt saying "Now I Can Die in Peace" That's how I feel about this opportunity to have my say with regard to our revolution. On the revolution, I think there are three things that are required for success. First is a just cause (draining the swamp), second is leadership which we have, maybe not George Washington but the best available today. The third is a large percentage of the people who are willing to follow, here Trump leads Washington. We the people must stand by our President and his agenda to impose real change to government for and by we the people. We must demonstrate to the world how government should function for the benefit of all the people equally. I've always thought that Truth Will Set Us Free and it could be a peaceful revolution if the people are well informed. It's our job to keep them informed.

No one knows for certain how this will all turn out. I've taken an optimistic view because in our past our nation has mostly chosen the right path. We have once again been blessed with the opportunity to make an improvement to our nation. On the bright side in my opinion we have only one major hurdle to overcome and that's our government-imposed lack of equality. We the people have to use this flaw as our rallying point to help President Trump in his quest to end corruption.

On the not so encouraging side there is the problem of our human nature. It's long been my opinion that about 90% of us are not capable of leadership and are dependent on those who are. What we must overcome is the problem that the majority who are able have not been holding the One % who have been looking out for themselves accountable. If you do the math, we are 30 odd million strong and have a responsibility to do what is right for the other 300 million who are counting on our leadership.

As I come to the close of this book, I have to make a comment on what is happening now. For the past few years there has been a great interest on what is termed global warming or climate change and what man's influence has been. As I write today, we have had the hurricane in Texas and Florida is in the sights of Irma. Rest assured we humans had nothing to do with it. We don't have power over nature, God does. In the past there have been floods, earthquakes and other destruction that we didn't cause.

Now those who don't believe in or know about God may ask how could a just God allow this to happen? They may never see the truth because they don't believe. I'm going to try to help. We humans are very interested in our personal appearance and the impression we make on others. God has no interest in what we look like, only what we actually do with this body we have. None of us will be taking it with us. God's interest is in what we have done with it to praise him and help each other. It's all about saving our soul that will be leaving here to join God if that is God's will. Your body isn't going anywhere, just back to dust.

I believe God is providing us with yet another opportunity to demonstrate our willingness to put ourselves second and do everything we can to help others. It's where I began and where I'll end with this plea that we bring God and righteousness back into our nation.

With the natural disasters comes the good and the bad. The good being the examples of one American helping another who is in need. The bottom of the barrel is those who would loot. This brings to my attention the organizations that are nonprofits that are supposed to be charitable providers. This is a subject that I have avoided in the past. However, the issue is now in the news. In the wake of the Houston hurricane, Houston City Councilman Dave Martin made a comment on the subject regarding the American Red Cross." I beg you not to send them a penny, they are the most inept unorganized organization I've ever experienced". I believe Mr. Martin was being kind.

Here's my opinion of the ARC. It starts with a talk I had with an uncle when I was maybe 12 years old sitting alone in our back yard. He was telling me about his life in NY and his good fortune. He told me he had many years ago done some favor for Lucky Luciano (I have no idea what it could have been). He claimed that he had been rewarded with a no-show position at White Rock which was a beverage company. On talking of his great life, he said he had a couple of neighbors who he fished and played golf with. They both were former political figures who were district directors of the Red Cross. Does Elizabeth Dole ring a bell?

Years later when I was in the Army in Berlin, there was a notice that it was Red Cross month and the CO wanted us to have 100 % participation in donations. I refused and was sent to see the deputy CO where I explained that I would never contribute to the Red Cross. They claimed 100 % donations but I didn't give anything. Three years later we had a Sargent arrive at our company. I was getting ready to leave and he was interested in my off-post apartment. He was awaiting the arrival of his wife whom he had married in Korea. He told me that he had been on a troop ship from Korea to California when his cabin was broken into and his money stolen. When he arrived in California he went to the Red Cross for help. The Red Cross gave him two bus tickets to his home town in Washington and $20 cash but they required that he sign a consent that they would be reimbursed in full from his next paycheck. The next year I was ending my enlistment at Valley Forge General Hospital in Pa. The patients were mostly those with injuries from Viet Nam. On Saturday nights the Red Cross came through selling cigarettes and sandwiches to the patients. The Salvation Army heard of this and started coming through an hour earlier giving sandwiches away free. We didn't see the Red Cross again. In the mean time we have this organization with a monopoly on our nation's blood supply. They freely accept the blood and granted there is some expense in obtaining and processing it but rest assured when the Red Cross parts with it someone is going to pay. Be very leery of any organization that is closely associated with the government. As the old saying goes, birds of a feather flock together.

I need to interject one more observation. I love our American History warts and all. What I've noticed are the people who have chosen to align with President Trump. Dr. Ben Carson, former Speaker and historian Newt Gingrich, Mike Pence and most importantly our military leaders. These are some of our best and brightest and we should follow their lead.

I made a decision decade ago that I didn't like the direction that our government was leading us. I particularly don't like the loss of freedom. Most seem willing to put up with it. When cell phones came along, I didn't care for the idea that anyone could call me at anytime so I bought one and put it in my drawer to be used only when I was going out of town so that I could call AAA in case I needed them. I've never answered a cell phone call. It goes without saying that I don't have a smart phone that informs the government everywhere I've been and where I am now. I've determined that I write in protest with little hope of it being a financial success, just to feel that I've done something to spread truth in a world of deception.

For my closing statement made nine months into President Trumps first year. There has been some success. The Supreme Court appointment and the stock market and economy are headed in a positive direction. The failure of repeal and replace was a learning experience for the President in that he should never trust the words of the establishment which is against him no matter which party they claim to represent. Recently Tom Price had to resign for continuation with business as usual when Trump is looking to play a new game that includes looking after the people's money and how it is supposed to be handled. There can be little trust in anyone who has been too long in office or government service. They are very unlikely to accept the new direction that we as a nation must head if we are to survive.

Before I forget, I hope that the President comes to realize that Jeff Sessions as AG is a mistake and has to go ASAP. He seems all too willing to overlook political corruption and will never hold Eric Holder or the Clintons accountable. The President needs to fire him and replace him with an interim AG to perform a total house cleaning at the Justice Department, as a starting point anyone who is not with the new program should be rewarded with a transfer to Chicago to guard the Obama Library.

I firmly believe that God has his ways and has given us a chance to all pull together because of the terrible hurricane season we've had to face. We can see that there is no shortage of American spirit with regard to helping each other as is God's intention.

Puerto Rico is a problem in that it was in terrible financial shape before the hurricane disasters. The people holding Puerto Rico's debt will try to recoup by taking advantage of this mess. They need to be made an example of and prosecuted.

We've been given this opportunity to change direction back toward being the moral and righteous country we were intended to be. It all starts with draining the swamp. The President is presenting his vision to the people and they are going to respond. The establishment will try everything in their power to impede his efforts. It's up to us to clear the path by eliminating the position of career politician. As the old saying goes "Remember in November". We need to have both political parties to go broke supporting incumbent candidates. This can only happen if we get righteous volunteers. The McConnells and Shumers of our current system need to be remembered as relics of a failed past that didn't represent the needs of all the people equally.

The Senate currently does nothing, the House has at least passed hundreds of bills that are just languishing in the do nothing Senate. We clearly need a major change in the Senate to shake the rust off and get the wheels back in motion.

The world is changing at light speed but our government is sitting on their hands as if nothing important is happening. As with so many things today they are obsolete. We have a window to make change with as little turbulence as possible. I believe that manual labor will be almost totally gone in twenty years. Robots will be doing most everything. In the mean time we must repair our neglected infrastructure. This will provide work and meaning for those who are still in the labor force.

We must look to the future where there is likely to be little or no labor force and how we may best run our country. The President is seeking tax cuts to stimulate the economy and that's OK but we really need a total tax reform such as the "Fair Tax". I know that the left despite their good intentions will never understand their lack of equality. Theft will never be the correct answer for anything.

If anyone out there doesn't understand that we are being challenged you are not paying attention to anything outside your daily requirements for existence. It's time to wake up America. God has dropped the ball into our court. The question is what are we going to do with it?

In looking around this planet, consider the world situation. We have these elitists, mostly white men who think we shouldn't be allowed to get along without them being in charge. Check out Africa a mostly black continent. Massive starvation and what have they done there? Try to protect the wild life. In our own country they have ignored the plight in Chicago, after all it's just blacks killing blacks. We the people must get rid of them and their puppets.

I'm back to life in 2019 after a mostly lost 2018. My wife and I were watching Leonard Cohan in concert in London on CD the other day. One of the tunes stated everything has a crack in it, that's how the light gets in. It brought me to understand that is my wanted place. I'd like to be the crack that lets the truth into our country. I can see now that I was overly optimistic with regard to the 2018 elections.

Let's light up our major problems. Debt is at the head of the list. The Congress has no will to address this problem because of its cause. We don't have balanced budgets that address the debt. They pay the interest and keep kicking the principle down the road and adding more to it. The major cause of the debt is promises made that should never have happened.

Social Security and Medicaid are personal responsibility where the government has no business but once started, free stuff is hard to end.

The solution for an end to this is to take nothing away from anyone now living. An end date must be established say July 2076. Mandatory health saving and personal retirement accounts for every worker should start asap. Those within fifteen years of age sixty-five should be exempted. Those between sixteen and twenty-five years should be offered a choice. Every worker must save 5% of their earnings for retirement and 2.5% for health savings. Every employer must match these accounts monthly. Both employers and employees may choose a higher number if agreed to by both sides.

About the Federal Budget, it should start each year with the interest on the debt and a matching amount on the principle. This and the military are required along with the judicial system. They should have reduction in force of government employees due to turning programs over to the states.

I'm very happy with the 2019 State of the Union speech. I'm elated that the liberal media had to report that 75% of the people approved.

Disappointed that the Conmess is fighting with the President over our border defense. We really need to get rid of politics and on to well-run government that is in our best interest.

Over the last fifty years or so, I've read many books and articles on freedom. None more enlightening than The Law by Frederic Bastiat [1801-1850]. I discovered that much of my current beliefs stem from this French economist, who was at the time of the French revolution, espousing in his writings the virtues of freedom. He was a distinct minority during his life time but the history of our country during the following century points out the correctness of his positions. In this book he quotes Billaud Varennes;" A people who are to be returned to liberty must be formed anew. A strong force and vigorous action are necessary to destroy old prejudices, to change the old customs, to correct depraved affections, to resist superfluous wants and destroy ingrained vices."

This is where we are today, on the verge of liberty lost and the only way to save it is to return to a state of little government and citizen leadership devoid of professional politicians. The most important event of the past five hundred years was our revolution and we are about to destroy it. The founders warned us that we had to throw the government out every so often and renew our leadership. The time has come where silence is no longer acceptable. This book is a call for action.

The lord presented us with a republic and we're screwing it up by being ungrateful. It's all about the mishandling of authority problem. We've let the rule of man get the upper hand.

Let's look at the ninety percent sheeple as sheep who need to be cared for. We of the nine percent have stood by being puppies. We are happy and content and living the good life and not worrying about the flock. We started with one percent shepherds in charge but we've allowed them to be replaced by the wolf class. The flock is shrinking and the wolves are large, fat, happy and growing in numbers. We are not thinking about the wolves because they have never been a problem for us puppies. There are still plenty of sheep and the wolves are content with their freezers full of lamb. If we don't start paying attention to this problem, we will be facing the day when the flock is just skeletons and the wolves will change their eating habits to include puppy. Our responsibility is driving off the class and restoring the shepherds once again.

We are in danger of having the wolves institute the European Socialist way of running our country in place of the republic that we started with. In the socialist systems God doesn't come into the picture. It's all about doing things by the rule of man and we're not capable of ruling ourselves without the wolves to keep us in line.

God has Trumped America and we must take advantage of our blessing and be thankful we are still receiving God's help. Step up do your share, your children and grandchildren are counting on you. We have more people working so the time is right to have a large switch on how the future finances of the people is addressed, we should all carry our own responsibility and be able to pass it on to our family members. We are still the greatest nation on earth but we living today didn't make it. It has been inherited and we are on the verge of blowing our inheritance to the new world order that would have them lead the world to be one giant Venezuela. We have allowed corrupt leadership and it's up to us to fix the problem. The answer is simple enough, equality for all, preference for none.

We currently have veteran's preference. I'm a veteran and would now and throughout my life have preferred equality for all as our national standard. What we owe our veterans is the opportunity to be equal to everyone else, especially if they are disabled.

We've become quite lazy as a nation. There are just too many of us who are content to accept the government dole, rather than fend for themselves. We need to help them out by eliminating the federal dole programs. The states should be in charge of all welfare and disability programs.

We the people must elect representatives who are in favor of equality for all. These would be temporary servants not career politicians.

May God continue to bless America. Let it be so. Amen.

www.ingramcontent.com/pod-product-compliance
Ingram Content Group UK Ltd.
Pitfield, Milton Keynes, MK11 3LW, UK
UKHW022219230426
12048UKWH00016BA/946